Morphē
A Journey of
Architectural Inspiration

Van Damme • Vandeputte Architects

LUSTER

- **To create good architecture one must get to know the setting inside and out.**
-

Morphē: A Journey of Architectural Inspiration

Welcome to **Morphē**, a unique chronicle that reflects our collective experiences and passion for architecture. Architecture courses through our veins; we wake up and fall asleep with it. With this book, we set sail on a voyage of introspection, unveiling our body of work, our world of existence, and the wellspring of our inspiration to the world.

This book goes beyond the confines of a conventional architectural portfolio, transcending the boundaries of a documentary overview of our projects. Instead, **Morphē** is a carefully crafted diary, a compendium of our thoughts and musings on the transformative power of architecture that has shaped our lives.

At its core, the title **Morphē**, encapsulates the very essence of our architectural philosophy. Derived from the Greek word meaning 'form' or 'shape,' **Morphē** symbolises the infinite potential for change and metamorphosis inherent in our creations. Just like a caterpillar undergoes a radical transformation to emerge as a magnificent butterfly, architecture can reshape our environments, enhance our experiences, and evoke deep emotions.

Morphē is a celebration of our achievements and an invitation to join us on this never-ending quest for architectural excellence. Take a voyage with us through the realms of architecture as we delve deeper into the very essence of our work. This book gives readers an insight into the vibrant tapestry of our creative process, with inspirational images of finished projects and renders of projects we are working on. It unveils the secrets of our architectural practice, offering glimpses into the everyday world of our office. Each page reveals a new dimension, where ideas are nurtured, concepts are moulded, and dreams are brought to life.

Our captivating journey begins with an interview, which affords you a glimpse into the minds and perspectives of the architects behind the creations, larded with intimate anecdotes and personal reflections on the transformative power of architecture. By delving into our collective experiences, we seek to inspire seasoned professionals and budding enthusiasts alike, reminding everyone who engages with this book that architecture has the power to shape our world and our lives. From there, we traverse various architectural themes, with each chapter unveiling a unique facet of our design philosophy through carefully curated images that highlight our projects. This well-curated collection aims to ignite the imagination and provoke reflection. We end with some of the projects that are currently in the pipeline, of which we are particularly proud.

So, without further ado, turn the page and join us on this extraordinary journey. Let the words and images of **Morphē** kindle your imagination, open your mind to new possibilities, and leave an indelible mark on your creative spirit.

Hannes Van Damme and Benoît Vandeputte

Conversation is everything
P9

Silent statements
P23

A place & time continuum
P53

Inviting ambiance
P99

In the stillness of space
P141

From a rhythm to a flow
P169

Shaping tomorrow
P217

Conversation is everything

An inspiring interview with Hannes Van Damme & Benoît Vandeputte

By Iris De Feijter

"Books are the most beautiful monuments that one generation can leave to another. They are more enduring than buildings, more profound than philosophy, and more intimate than paintings", said Le Corbusier. A statement that Hannes Van Damme (b. 1989, pictured left) and Benoît Vandeputte (b. 1989, pictured right) wholeheartedly endorse. Since founding their architecture firm in 2018, they have carved out a legacy with a portfolio that includes dozens of homes, offices, and shops in Belgium and abroad. This book now adds a new dimension with a curated selection of projects that are each indicative of the architects' oeuvre in their own way.

In publishing this book, the fledgling architecture firm reveals its ambition. Similarly, the new headquarters of Van Damme • Vandeputte attest to their shared vision. The firm recently moved into an old doctor's practice and home in Izegem after renovating the classicist building with the utmost care and respect for its history. They even purposefully preserved the domestic atmosphere in their office, designing an open kitchen with a bar for use by the firm's employees in addition to an inviting seating area for client meetings with comfortable seating, inspiring books, and a sculpture by young Belgian artist Florian Tomballe. "A homely look and feel is a vital aspect of our work, both in our residential or office designs", says Benoît Vandeputte.

Your firm is relatively new. Is publishing a book at this stage an indication of your ambition?
Hannes: Yes, we are newcomers, but it's worth noting that we have already completed a wide range of projects since our inception in 2018. A book is just the right medium for reflecting on our journey to date. Benoît and I love books, which explains the large library in our office. We leapt at the opportunity when Luster approached us to produce a book. We had to limit ourselves, selecting just 12 of the more than 50 projects in our portfolio to highlight them in great detail. However, our aim with this monograph was to do more than showcase our achievements. The design process is equally important. By including ongoing projects, this book also gives readers a better idea of how our projects come to fruition.
Benoît: The book also allowed us to reflect on our work and identity, to philosophise on architecture in general.

Can you tell us what characterises your designs?
Hannes: We don't like labels because our oeuvre includes very large and small-scale projects and everything in between. We specialise in architecture, interiors, shops, offices, and residential projects. What all our designs have in common, however, is humility. We don't believe in imposing a specific style on a client. Nor do we push through a spectacular design because it will boost our portfolio. Instead, we aim always to offer the right answer to the client's design brief. And we firmly believe in quality in everything we do.
Benoît: As an architect, you are also very much like a therapist, reconciling the wishes of different parties.
Hannes: Architecture is a living organism, which changes continuously over time. Likewise, we constantly adapt and tweak our views and vision. This ongoing process usually takes place during our hour-long car journeys or site visits in other countries. I think those are the most fascinating conversations.

What makes your approach unique? Have you defined a methodology? In other words, what happens after a client reaches out to you?
Benoît: The first conversation is actually the most important one in the entire collaboration. We spend hours discussing anything and everything to gauge whether we are a good match for each other. This is crucial because you are defining and shaping someone's living environment as an architect, something you can only do if you are on the same wavelength.
Hannes: It's all about the conversation. As an architect, your job is to build something for someone else. It's not about doing what you want. By constantly considering all the different aspects – the client's wishes, the existing situation, the budget, the regulations, the available materials – you demonstrate that you are really capable of designing something.

How do you start on a design? Is there a method?
Benoît: The cornerstone of many of our designs is the 'promenade architecturale', a concept devised by the Swiss architect Le Corbusier. It's like a miniature version of an old city like Paris or Venice, where narrow streets alternate with vast squares. We always try to include a variety of atmospheres and spaces in our designs to create a captivating walk.
Hannes: We want our clients to live in every space of their homes, which is why we create so many multi-purpose spaces. A space may serve as a living room during one stage of your life, after which it becomes a place to read or meditate, or even a studio. We often conceive dual-use spaces, such as a cosy reading corner for the evenings in a room that also has a breakfast corner. Sometimes we also add blank areas or undefined spaces, such as a staircase with long treads where you can sit and leaf through a book. Or a spacious room for your pottery or to host a Christmas dinner for twenty, that can also be used as a guest room.

Le Corbusier is an iconic figure both in architecture and furniture design. How has he influenced your practice, and what aspects of his work resonate with you?
Hannes: Le Corbusier and his cousin Pierre Jeanneret revolutionised modern architecture. Their impact is undeniable. Their pursuit of functionality, rationality, and the integration of art in architecture has profoundly influenced our approach. We admire their ability to create spaces that prioritise human needs and well-being while embracing innovative construction techniques and materials.
Benoît: We find their exploration of the relationship between furniture and architecture particularly inspiring as they recognised the importance of designing furniture that complemented their architectural vision. But their functional aesthetic also became a hallmark. We strive to create holistic spaces where the boundaries between architecture and furniture become blurred, just like Le Corbusier and Jeanneret did.
Hannes: Unfortunately, Le Corbusier's ideas for urban planning concepts failed. In that sense, we would hope that we can do better.

•
The pursuit of functionality, rationality, and the integration of art in architecture has profoundly influenced our approach.
•

Speaking of the built environment, which role do the environment and the 'genius loci' play in your designs?
Hannes: The location and the client's wishes are primordial. We try to spend as much time on-site as possible. We are currently working on a project on the shores of Lake Maggiore in Italy. We've been there ten times now, in all seasons. Only when you know the place inside and out can you create a good design.
Benoît: When the fog lifts in the morning, you can see the Swiss mountain peaks, so we added a window to frame this view. We also gazed out onto the water at night to see which villages in the area were beautifully lit, adjusting the evening spaces accordingly. By being on-site, you know, for example, which trees need to be felled to preserve the view. You can't see this on Google Street View or Skype.

How far do you go in terms of detail in your initial design? Is it a sketch that evolves as the process progresses? Or are these designs very elaborate, leaving little margin for improvisation and imagination?
Hannes: We put a lot of time and effort into the initial concept because we want to present our client with a design that is as complete and well-thought-through as possible at an early stage. So our initial design already includes the façades, the interior, the materials, the furniture, the landscaping, and even some suggestions about the placement of art and decorative objects. We use high-quality 3D visualisations and sketches for this, in which you can even see the finish of the walls and the hinges of the cupboards. These images really capture the future atmosphere.
Benoît: Naturally, details are added during the process in consultation with the people who build our designs. We both love to visit the studios of craftsmen and artists.
Benoît: These visits offer us a unique opportunity to witness creativity in all its manifestations and give us a fresh perspective. We also develop a deep appreciation for materials, textures, and the art of making something. We believe that architecture is an amalgam of various disciplines, and by immersing ourselves in the world of artists and craftsmen, we can broaden our own creative horizons. Our recent collaboration with Antwerp sculptor Florian Tomballe is a good example. We are working on various projects together and are obsessed with the abundant natural light in his studio. This luminous environment allows us to continually rediscover and appreciate the captivating allure of abstract shapes in his classical sculptures.

> **Our cooperation was born from our friendship and a shared vision. We think alike on many topics.**

Hannes: Such encounters also inspire us to add elements of craftsmanship to our designs. Whether incorporating bespoke furniture or collaborating with skilled artisans, we always strive to add a human touch and soul to our designs. By merging the worlds of art, craft, and architecture, we create spaces that resonate on a deeper level with those who inhabit them.
Benoît: Our visit to the workshops of Chapo Creations in Gordes was an amazing experience. Nadia, the companion of Fidel (Pierre Chapo's late son), took us on a tour of the original showroom and workshop, where we were able to see the legacy and craftsmanship of the renowned furniture designer first-hand. Spending time in this space where the southern French light flows in through the windows, surrounded by Chapo's beautiful creations, and experiencing the devotion to quality and detail left an indelible mark on us.
Hannes: It was a potent reminder that architecture and furniture design are intrinsically linked. Pierre Chapo's work embodied the essence of timelessness and reminded us of the importance of embracing traditional techniques while pushing boundaries to create something new. We left the atelier inspired and determined to introduce this philosophy into our own architectural endeavours.

Let's go back to the very beginning: before becoming partners in your firm, you already were firm friends. What inspired you to work together?
Benoît: We met while studying architecture at Sint-Lucas in Ghent and became good friends early on. We visited exhibitions in museums and galleries together, something we still do now. During these outings, we developed a shared reference framework.
Hannes: Our cooperation was born from our friendship and a shared vision. We think alike on many topics. We both love books. And when we visit an exhibition, we often single out the same things.
Benoît: We always visit the Venice Biennale of Architecture together. During one of our past trips, we set aside some time to take another look at the work of Carlo Scarpa, who was a true master in terms of blending craftsmanship and architectural design. His meticulous attention to detail and the poetic quality of his work resonate deeply with us. We appreciate how Scarpa created spaces that engage the senses, where materials and textures are carefully selected and celebrated. His integration of historical elements into contemporary designs is remarkable, something we strive to emulate in our projects.
Hannes: It's also a reminder that architecture should respect and respond to its context, embracing the layers of history and culture surrounding it. Scarpa's work encourages us to approach each project while being sensitive to the existing fabric and finding innovative ways to introduce new life while preserving the essence of a place.

You have worked on historical buildings and even listed monuments. How do you go about planning contemporary interventions in these cases?
Benoît: We always take a holistic approach, seeking to strike a balance between contemporary and historical elements, a perennial dilemma for architects working on restoration projects. It reminds me of the opposing ideas of John Ruskin and Viollet-le-Duc. For Viollet-le-Duc, something needed to be restored to a state that might never have fully existed but represented an ideal image. Ruskin, meanwhile, preferred an 'honest' restoration, with all the stages of the building process remaining visible in the finished project. Take Notre Dame de Paris, where they are now restoring the wooden trusses as part of the new roof. In Reims, they chose to build a concrete structure after the fire in the cathedral, just like in Antwerp's St. Paul's Church. I prefer the latter option. With sufficient respect for the existing heritage, obviously. The contrast

should never be such that it grates. I take my lead from David Chipperfield in that respect, who always succeeds in creating a masterful blend of new and old architecture. At the Neues Museum in Berlin, he succeeded in preserving the subtleties of the 19th-century building, which had sustained severe damage during the war, in combination with contemporary additions. He sees no need for grand gestures, preferring small, purposeful interventions instead.
Hannes: David Chipperfield's work is a testament to the importance of context and the power of simplicity. We greatly admire his ability to seamlessly blend contemporary design with historical environments, allowing the new to enhance and enrich the old. His approach resonates with our own philosophy of creating architecture that becomes a part of the surroundings rather than overpowering them.
Benoît: Chipperfield's work also underscores the idea of timelessness. Rather than being dictated by fleeting trends, his designs choose to stand the test of time. We appreciate his commitment to creating enduring architecture that will remain relevant and cherished for years.

Did you establish your firm right after graduating?
Benoît: Initially, we each went our own way. I completed a master's degree in conservation of monuments and sites in Leuven in 2016. My thesis on 'Adriaan Martens and Henry Van de Velde' won the thesis prize and was published by Stichting Kunstboek. After Hannes and I competed individually on the same projects, we decided in January 2018 to join forces and work together instead of competing against each other.
Hannes: I went to New York to work on my thesis and spent some time there. Eventually, I was offered a job with Michael Sorkin, working in the firm's theoretical research department. I then moved to an American architectural firm that provides support to architects for their overseas projects. I contributed to projects by Vincent Van Duysen, among others, transposing his concept and sketches into concrete plans and working with local contractors and artisans. I was also responsible for the on-site follow-up.

What brought you back to Belgium?
Hannes: A private developer asked me to design a multifamily dwelling with several stacked volumes, a commission for which I was given free rein. I felt this opportunity was too good to pass up. While New York is an amazing city, I soon realised that I would never be able to establish my own design office there. To become a 'registered architect', I would have had to start from scratch, obtaining an architecture degree in the US. Being away for five years made me realise how interesting Belgium is in terms of architecture. We may not be a big country, but we have produced a lot of high-quality architecture and have a solid international reputation. And now we are working abroad ourselves...

Can you tap into your American experience in Belgium?
Hannes: Yes. But the main thing I learned in the US is their attention to detail. They spend as much time and attention on the minor aspects of a project – such as the veneer of a watch or cigar safe – as the façade or the architectural structure, for example. Everything is talked through from A to Z with the entire team.

Why did you dream of becoming an architect? And what makes you so complementary?
Hannes: I am mainly fascinated by the technical side of architecture, the construction and the materials. Thanks to my thesis, my time in the US, and the research for my PhD, I developed an interest in urban planning and the role of public spaces in the city and society.
Benoît: My love of architecture comes from a very different place. I grew up in a family where art and antiques were important. Latin and aesthetics further nurtured my love of culture. I even considered studying art sciences. But ultimately, I ended up settling on architecture because I used to tear out articles from magazines in my spare time and design imaginary houses.

•

Being away for five years made me realise how interesting Belgium is in terms of architecture. We may not be a big country, but we have produced a lot of high-quality architecture.

•

What have you learned from each other?
Benoît: We are the ideal pairing. I tend to be more focused on aesthetics, while Hannes's technical background serves me well on a daily basis.
Hannes: Benoît has a vast art-historical knowledge, a rewarding library that I love to draw from for inspiration. But he also knows a lot about materials and the crafts behind them, from carpet weaving to yarn spinning.
Benoît: Books are our number one source of inspiration. I already have more in my library than I will be able to read in a lifetime. I have lots of theoretical works on architecture and especially art books, rather than coffee-table books. Artists may work in a different medium, but I incorporate many of their elements into my architecture, like the unique framing of Raoul De Keyser's paintings, focusing on a specific detail, or Sol Le Witt, who understood how to create an extra dimension by adding geometric shapes to the wall.
Hannes: That is exactly how I feel about James Turrell. He creates an additional dimension with shapes, light and colours, often combined with a view of the outside world. This makes me think about the traditional boundaries between art and architecture.

A book is a good time to look back. But above all, it is also a good time to end a chapter and cautiously look ahead at what the future may bring. What are your plans for the firm?
Hannes: Our goal is definitely not more staff or more turnover. Although we can comfortably accommodate a workforce of 25 employees in our offices, we only have 10. A clear evolution in the past year is the fact that we are now working on international projects, including a holiday home in the south of France, a flat in Paris, and a house in Italy. But we have found that international clients who are looking to build in Belgium have also found us, such as a Swiss company for whom we are designing a large office.

•

We would like to do more of our own projects, where we are both architect and builder, like when we built our own offices. You can go even further in terms of your concept.

•

What kind of projects are on your bucket list for the next few years? What is your ultimate dream project?
Benoît: Recently, we created a preliminary design for a private museum. Ultimately, the project didn't materialise but I hope to have the opportunity to design an art space one day.
Hannes: I would like to do more of my own projects, where we are both architect and builder, like when we built our own offices. You can go even further in terms of your concept, unlike when you're working for a client. Unfortunately, this is rather unusual in Belgium.
Benoît: We have come to a point where we can afford to be selective. We prefer to work on all-in projects, designing the architecture, the interior and the furnishings. Another ambition is to have enough time as part of our busy schedule to continue to find inspiration. I really need the input, the stimulation.

Silent statements

•

There's no need to shout when the message is clear. Good architecture is subtle, thoughtful, modest, emphasising the quality of the materials and the design rationale. Sophistication and comfort don't call for extravagant displays: the humblest creations can be the most unforgettable.

•

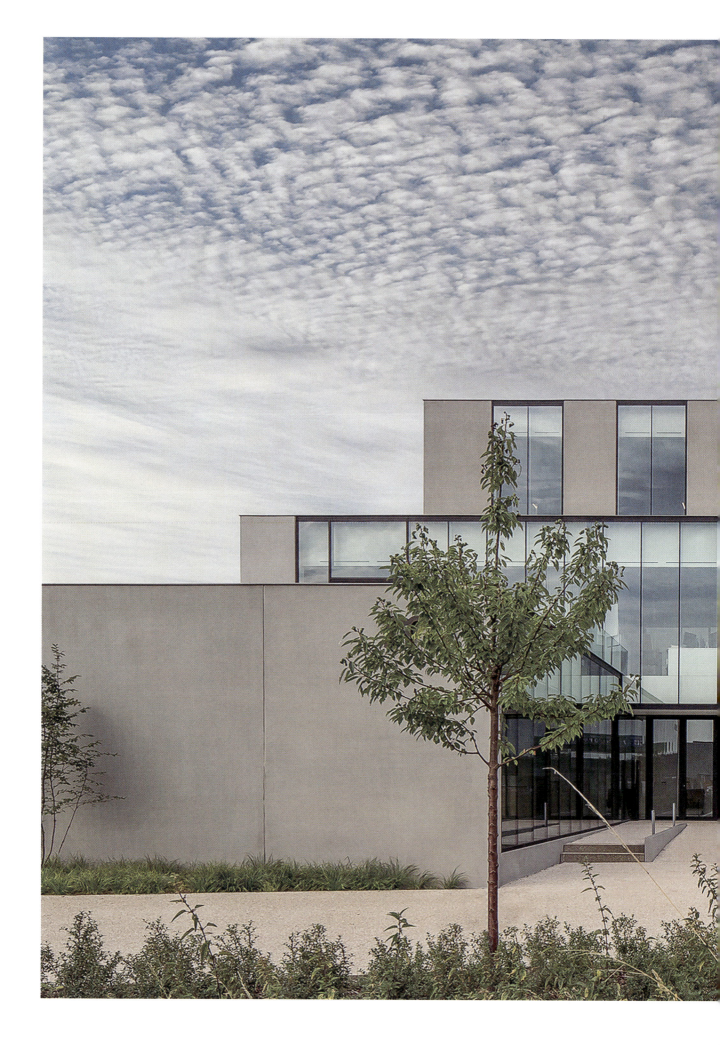

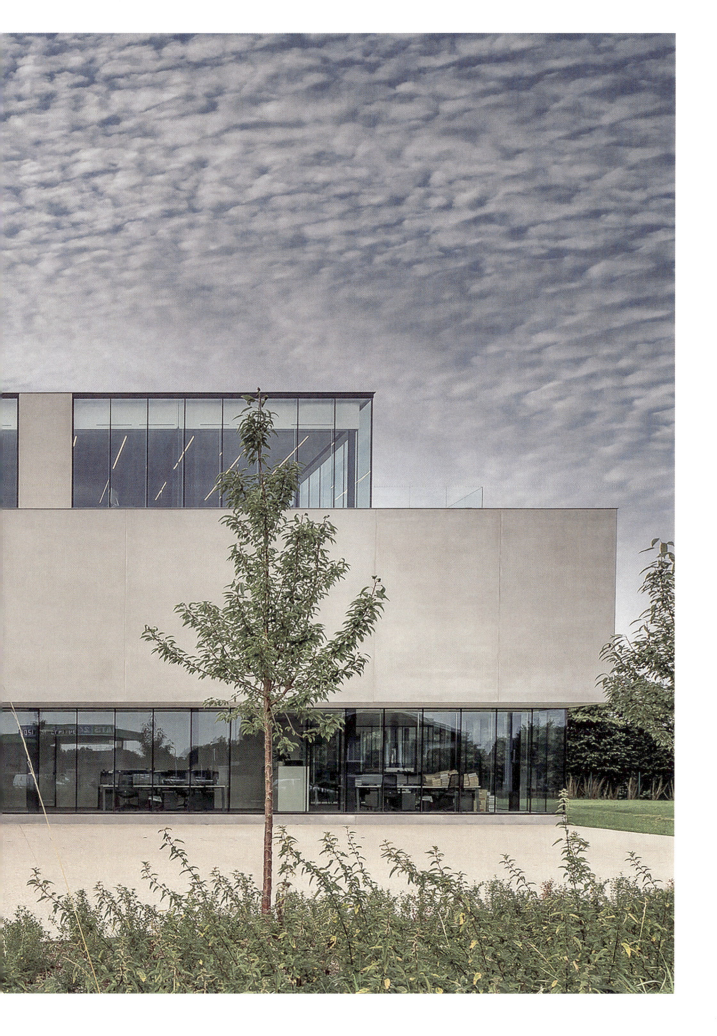

•
Spaces have the power to influence how we feel and behave.
•

A place & time continuum

•

No building is an island; every creation is surrounded by layers of history and culture. When architecture engages with its surroundings, a balance is achieved between the past and the present. Creating architecture implies a commitment to the past as well as the present. But more than anything else, it's a commitment to the future.

•

•
Every structure tells a story, reflecting its time and purpose.
•

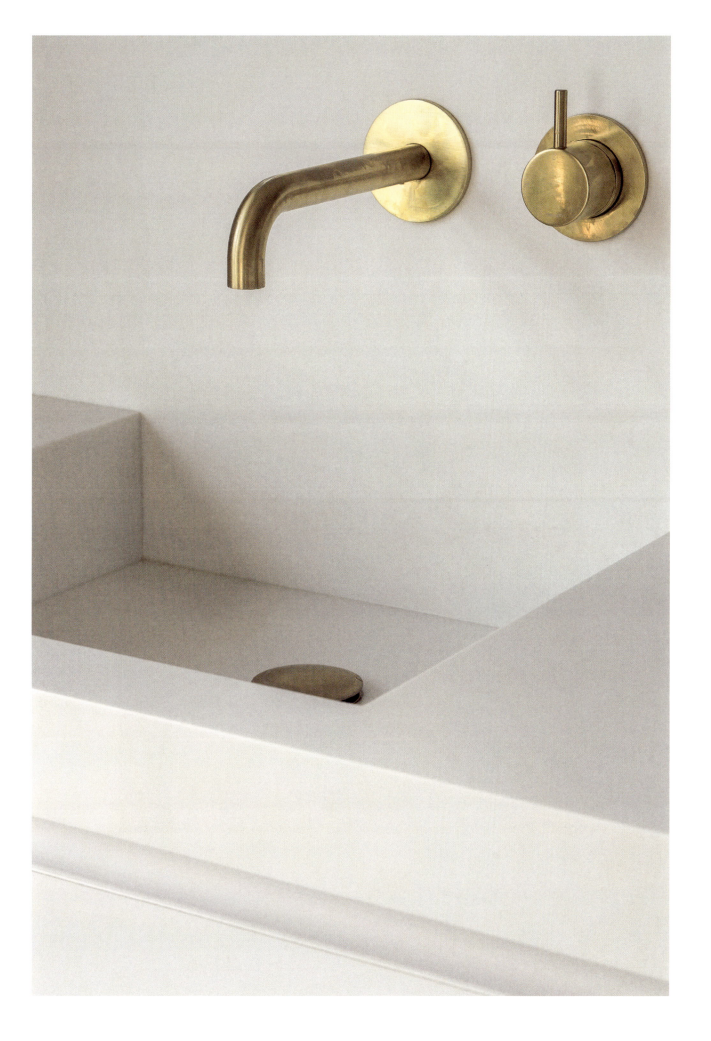

Inviting ambiance

•

There may be no place like home, but every space can – and should – feel like it. A good architect has excellent people skills, understanding human nature and sensing where his or her clients unwind. A good design feels like a warm embrace, for residents and visitors alike. All-in projects, in which the interior design and architecture are complimentary, are enriching in that sense. The message in each space is: you're welcome.

•

101

Through light, architecture finds its true character.

125

127

In the stillness of space

•

A building is a living and breathing organism, but time can feel like it has been stopped in its tracks in the architectural details. By paying attention to refined features, selecting tactile materials, and never compromising on quality, you can set the scene, creating an architectural instant that invites you to focus and be present. That is when true beauty reveals itself as being ever present and fleeting at the same time.

•

Spaces should inspire, comfort, and connect.

# From a rhythm to a flow

•

The way in which a building invites movement colours its soul. This movement – of people, of light, of air, of life – is the translation of a rhythm, which in turn is a translation of the shapes and volumes that are created during the design process. Whether geometric or abstract, rounded or sharp… Without form, there can be no content.

•

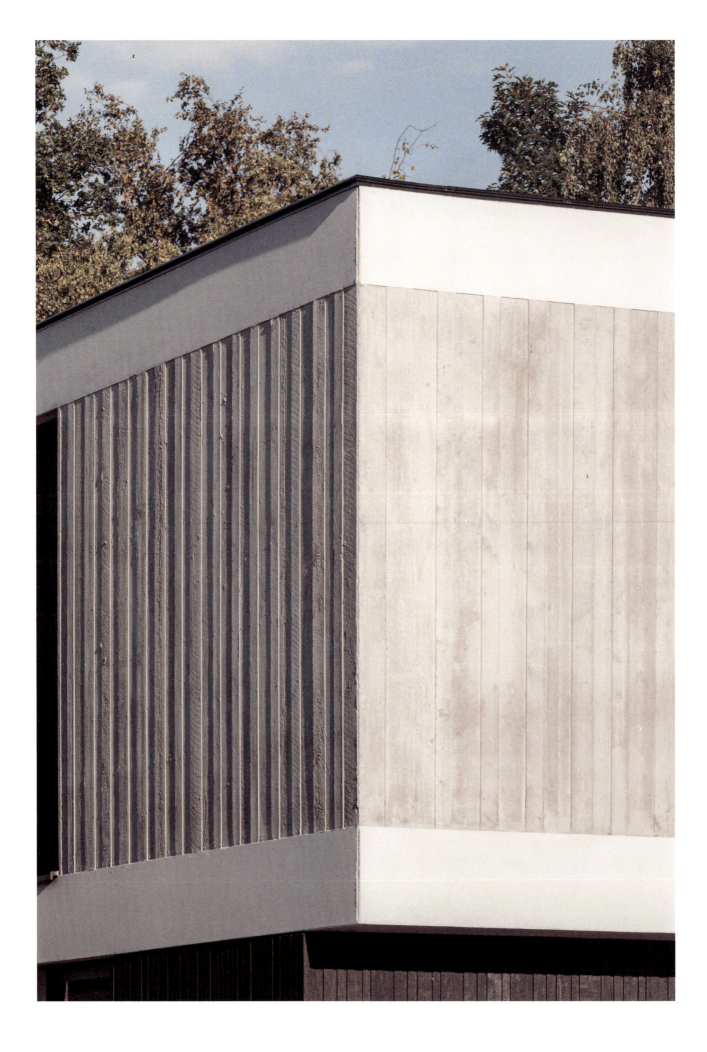

181

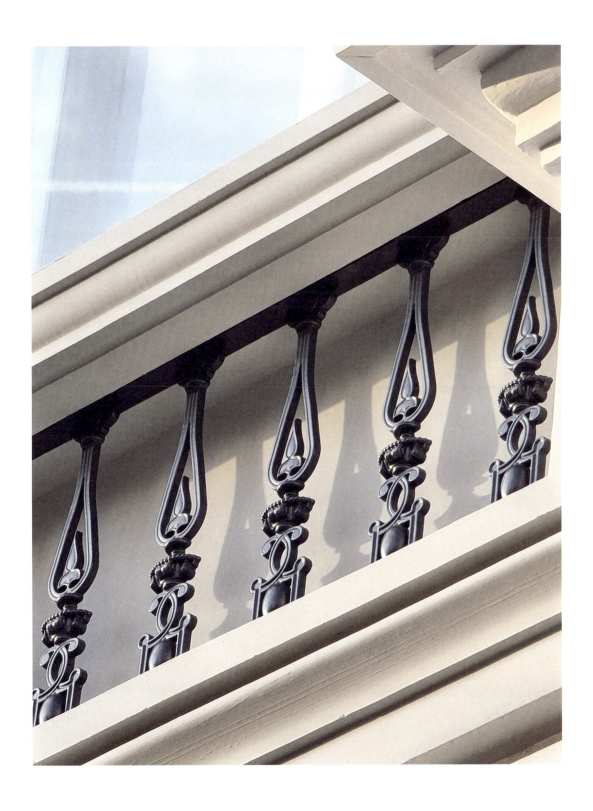

183

197

• Architecture is the outward expression of an inner essence.
•

Shaping tomorrow

•

Thinking about tomorrow's architecture goes hand-in-hand with wanting to move forward. Be that as it may, future projects only exist by the grace of moments of reflection. Because it is only over time that an architectural philosophy can mature into a vision of the things that are yet to come. Dreams shape the future, but the reverse is equally true: the future brings our dreams to life.

•

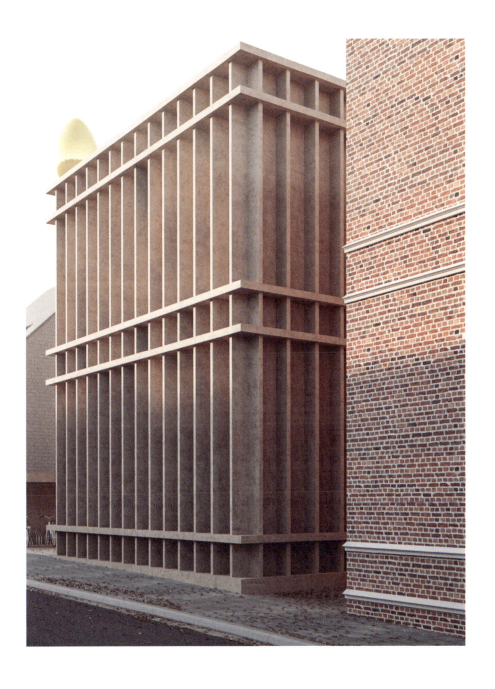

225

232

Index photography

P2: Offices VDVA
Photography by Cafeïne
P5: House 4D
Photography by Cafeïne
P8-13: Portrait Benoît & Hannes
Photography by Keen
P14-15: Studio Boquita de Cielo
Photography by Giannina Urmeneta
P17: Offices VDVA, details
Photography by Keen
P18: Hullebusch
Photography by Cafeïne
P20: Marble
Photography by Keen
P21: Atelier Florian Tomballe
Photography by Van Damme • Vandeputte
P22: House 4D
Photography by Van Damme • Vandeputte
P24-25: Offices VDVA
Photography by Cafeïne
P26-27: House VV
Photography by Cafeïne
P28-29: House DV
Photography by Van Damme • Vandeputte
P30-31: Offices VDVA
Photography by Cafeïne
P33: House AVV
Photography by Cafeïne
P34-35: Offices DG
Photography by Van Damme • Vandeputte
P36-37: Offices M1
Photography by Cafeïne
P38-39: Offices VDVA
Photography by Cafeïne
P40: House AVV, orchard
Photography by Van Damme • Vandeputte
P41: Offices VGDG
Photography by Cafeïne
P42: Residence R
Photography by Cafeïne
P44-45: Offices SU
Photography by Cafeïne
P47: House VDM
Photography by Cafeïne
P48: House AVV
Photography by Cafeïne
P49: Offices M1
Photography by Cafeïne
P50: Offices M1
Photography by Cafeïne
P51: Offices SU
Photography by Cafeïne
P52: House GM
Photography by All-Bouw
P54: House VTG, project site
Photography by Van Damme • Vandeputte
P55: Offices VDVA
Photography by Van Damme • Vandeputte

P56-57: Untitled by Boquita de Cielo
Photography by Keen
P58: House SA
Photography by Van Damme • Vandeputte
P60-61: Offices VDVA
Photography by Cafeïne
P62-63: Offices VDVA
Photography by Cafeïne
P64: Guildhouse GC
Photography by Keen
P66-67: House AVV
Photography by Cafeïne
P68: Tiger Onyx
Photography by Van Damme • Vandeputte
P71: Offices VDVA
Photography by Cafeïne
P72: House 4D
Photography by Cafeïne
P73: House VTG, project site
Photography by Van Damme • Vandeputte
P75: House 4D
Photography by Cafeïne
P76-77: Offices VDVA
Photography by Cafeïne
P79-82: House AVV
Photography by Cafeïne
P84: House AVV, summer border
Photography by Van Damme • Vandeputte
P85: House AVV
Photography by Cafeïne
P86: Offices VGDG
Photography by Cafeïne
P89: House SA
Photography by Van Damme • Vandeputte
P90-91: Residence R
Photography by Cafeïne
P93: Residence R
Photography by Cafeïne
P94: House VV
Photography by Cafeïne
P95: House 4D
Photography by Cafeïne
P96: House AVV
Photography by Cafeïne
P98: Offices VGDG
Photography by Cafeïne
P100-102: House 4D
Photography by Cafeïne
P103: House VV
Photography by Cafeïne
P104: Offices VGDG
Photography by Cafeïne
P106: House 4D
Photography by Cafeïne
P109: Offices VDVA
Photography by Cafeïne
P110: Offices VGDG
Photography by Cafeïne
P112-113: Offices VDV
Photography by Cafeïne

P114: House 4D
Photography by Cafeïne
P115: House AVV
Photography by Cafeïne
P116: Offices VD
Photography by Cafeïne
P119: House AVV
Photography by Cafeïne
P120-121: Offices VGDG
Photography by Gianni Vancompernolle
P122: House SA
Photography by Van Damme • Vandeputte
P123: House VDM
Photography by Cafeïne
P125-126: Offices VDVA
Photography by Cafeïne
P127: House 4D
Photography by Design Oostende
P128-129: House AVV
Photography by Cafeïne
P130: House VDM
Photography by Cafeïne
P133: Offices VDVA
Photography by Keen
P134: Offices VGDG
Photography by Cafeïne
P135: Offices VGDG
Photography by Cafeïne
P136: Offices VDV
Photography by Cafeïne
P139: Offices VGDG
Photography by Cafeïne
P140: Offices VDVA
Photography by Cafeïne
P142: House VDM
Photography by Cafeïne
P144: House VV
Photography by Cafeïne
P145: Offices VDVA
Photography by Cafeïne
P146: House 4D
Photography by Cafeïne
P148-149: Offices VDVA
Photography by Keen
P150: Offices VDVA, back door
Photography by Van Damme • Vandeputte
P151: House VDM
Photography by Cafeïne
P152-153: Offices VDVA
Photography by Cafeïne
P154-157: Offices VGDG
Photography by Cafeïne
P158: Offices VDVA
Photography by Cafeïne
P161: House VDM
Photography by Cafeïne
P162-165: Offices VDVA
Photography by Cafeïne
P166: Offices VGDG
Photography by Cafeïne

P168: House CL
Photography by Bert Demasure
P171: House VV
Photography by Cafeïne
P172-175: House VDM
Photography by Cafeïne
P176-177: House CL
Photography by Bert Demasure
P178: Kew gardens
Photography by Van Damme • Vandeputte
P180-181: House VDM
Photography by Studio Camade
P182: House GM
Photography by Van Damme • Vandeputte
P183: House SA
Photography by Van Damme • Vandeputte
P185: Offices VGDG
Photography by Cafeïne
P186-187: Residence R
Photography by Studio Camade
P189: Colonne by Alban Lanore
Photography by Cafeïne
P191: House 4D
Photography by Cafeïne
P192: House AVV, De geknielde jongeling
by George Minne
Photography by Cafeïne
P193: Offices VDVA
Photography by Cafeïne
P194: House VV
Photography by Cafeïne
P195: House AVV
Photography by Cafeïne
P196-197: Offices DG
Photography by Van Damme • Vandeputte
P198-199: House VDM
Photography by Studio Camade
P200: House 4D
Photography by Cafeïne
P202-206: Offices VDVA
Photography by Cafeïne
P209: Guildhouse GC
Photography by Van Damme • Vandeputte
P210-211: House 4D
Photography by Cafeïne
P213: House AVV
Photography by Cafeïne
P214-215: Offices VDVA
Photography by Cafeïne
P239: Portrait Hannes & Benoît
Photography by Keen

Index visualisation
by Van Damme • Vandeputte

P216: Offices HB
P218: Apartment LCH, Dining room,
Paris, France
P218: Offices DG, Lounge, Deinze
P219: House VK, Outdoor wellness,
Nieuwpoort
P219: House VK, Outside dining area,
Nieuwpoort
P220: House VTG, Lake side,
Lago Maggiore, Italy
P220: Offices FL, Courtyard, Roeselare
P221: City Hall K, West elevation,
Kruishoutem
P221: Apartment LCH, Living room,
Paris, France
P222: House DV, Rear view,
Oostduinkerke
P222: Residence VA, Rear view, Kortrijk
P223: House DN, Main entrance, Wingene
P223: Offices PD, Street façade,
Sint-Martens-Latem
P224: Offices HB, Main façade,
Roeselare
P224: UR Foundation, Main pavilion
P225: House GM, Garden wing,
Zwevegem
P225: Offices VI, Overall view, Roeselare
P226: House VG, Entrance view of
the villa, Gignese, Italy
P226: Apartment LCH, Kitchen,
Paris, France
P227: House DN, Garden side, Wingene
P227: UR Foundation, Entrance pavilion
P228: Offices HB, Showroom, Roeselare
P228: Residence D, Overall view, Koksijde
P229: House G, Front view of
the residence, Oostduinkerke
P229: Residence D, Overall view, Koksijde
P230-231: House VG, Rear view,
Gignese, Italy
P232: Offices DG, Main entrance, Deinze
P232: Offices FL, Street façade, Roeselare
P233: House DV, Main façade,
Oostduinkerke
P233: House VTG, Front view of
the residence, Lago Maggiore, Italy
P234: Offices AW, Main entrance, Tielt
P235: Apartment LCH, Living room,
Paris, France

Thank you

Our book is the result of a lot of dedication, creativity and collaboration. We would like to take this opportunity to express our sincere gratitude to all those who made this project possible.
First of all, we would like to thank our visionary clients. Their trust in our studio has inspired us to strive for excellence and innovation in every project we have been privileged to realise.
Your vision and enthusiasm have inspired and motivated us to push our boundaries time and again. We also would like to thank our talented team. Without their tireless efforts, creative genius, and continued dedication to the art of architecture, this book would not have been possible. Each of them played an invaluable role in shaping the projects presented in this book, and we are immensely grateful for their hard work and dedication.

Our deepest appreciation also goes to the indispensable artisans and artists we work with. They are the backbone of every project, contributing their skill and dedication and helping us turn our designs into tangible reality. Their technical expertise, craftsmanship, and determination have brought our visions to life and laid the foundation for the beautiful architecture we are proud to present today. Without good contractors, there can be no good project, and we are grateful for their partnership and cooperation. Their tireless efforts deserve credit, and we look forward to working on many more successful projects with them in the future.

We are also grateful to Iris De Feijter for turning our inspiring conversation into a text that truly represents our vision.

Last but not least, our deepest appreciation also goes to our publisher, Luster, and graphic designer, Bart Kiggen, whose belief in our work has led to the creation of this book. Their efforts and expertise have allowed us to share our projects with a broader audience and spread our passion for architecture.

Morphē
A Journey of Architectural Inspiration

A book by
Van Damme • Vandeputte Architects

Interview
Iris De Feijter

Translation
Sandy Logan

Editing
Hadewijch Ceulemans

Graphic design
Bart Kiggen

Images: see P236

D/2023/12.005/15
ISBN 9789460583575
NUR 648

© 2023 Van Damme • Vandeputte Architects
& Luster Publishing

info@vandammevandeputte.com
vandammevandeputte.com
@vandammevandeputte

info@lusterpublishing.com
lusterpublishing.com
@lusterbooks

All rights reserved. No part of this publication may be reproduced, stored in a retrieval system, or transmitted, in any form or by any means, without the prior written consent of the publisher. An exception is made for short excerpts, which may be cited for the sole purpose of reviews.